ALL ABOUT

Marie Curie

Claire Caprioli

BLUE RIVER PRESS

Indianapolis, Indiana

Published by Blue River Press
Indianapolis, Indiana
www.brpressbooks.com

Distributed by Cardinal Publishers Group
A Tom Doherty Company, Inc.
www.cardinalpub.com

ISBN: 978-1-68157-180-5

LCCN: 2021935107

Cover Design: David Miles
Book Design: Korab Company Design
Cover Artist: Nicole McCormick Santiago
Editor: Dani McCormick
Illustrator: Moriah McReynolds

Printed in the United States of America

10 9 8 7 6 5 4 3 2 1   21 22 23 24 25 26 27 28 29 30

CONTENTS

ALL ABOUT

Marie Curie

"I have been stupid. I am stupid and I shall remain stupid all the days of my life..."

These words were written by a young woman named Maria Sklodowska to her sister, Bronya. At the time, she was experiencing an emotion that we are all familiar with: self-doubt. Fortunately, Maria pushed past this emotion and became one of the most brilliant and famous scientists in the world. It's hard to believe that such a person could ever have thought that of herself.

Today we know Maria Sklodowska as Marie Curie.

Marie was born in 1867 to a Polish family in the city of Warsaw. The only problem was that Poland did not exist! Poland had been taken over by Germany, Russia, and Austria between 1772 and 1795. In 1863, Russian police, professors, and government officials were sent to Warsaw and other Russian-owned parts of Poland. Their job was to get rid of the Polish language, books, newspapers, history, and religion.

Marie had to work very hard her whole life. She was Polish, and the Russians discriminated against Poles. She was female and could not get a college education in her own country. Her family was poor, and she would study late into the night with no food or heat. Most of all, Marie had to work hard because she had chosen a challenging life of scientific discovery. Marie suffered many hardships and battled depression from a young age. And yet, Marie was also patient, determined, and persistent. In other words, she never gave up.

Marie's persistence allowed her to accomplish many things in her sixty-six years. She became the first woman to receive a Physics degree at the Sorbonne in France. She was the first female professor at the Sorbonne and the first woman admitted into the French Academy of Medicine. She discovered the elements polonium and radium. She became the first woman to receive a Nobel prize, and later, the first person of any gender to receive two Nobel Prizes. Oh, and along the way, she helped more than a million World War I soldiers!

But Marie Curie never set out to be famous or the first woman of anything. She followed her passion and didn't let anything, including self-doubt, stop her from achieving her goals.

To all those of Polish heritage. Be proud.

CHAPTER ONE

Early Childhood

On November 7, 1867, in a country that wasn't a country, a baby girl came into the world. Her parents named her Maria, and nicknamed her Manya. Manya's family had a proud Polish heritage, even though Poland had been under foreign rule for many years.

Manya (Marie) lived in Warsaw, which was under Russian rule at the time.

Manya's parents, Bronislawa (left) and Wladislaw (right) were very proud of their Polish hertiage.

In Warsaw, where Manya lived, the Russians were oppressive towards the Polish people, language, and customs. Polish rebels were easily stopped by the powerful Russian military.

The Polish people realized that they had to use their brains instead of their fists. It would take scholars, artists, priests, and teachers to influence future generations and keep Polish patriotism alive. It would take people like Manya's parents.

Manya's mother Bronislawa Sklodowska was an intelligent woman who had once been the director of a girls' school. She was a gray-eyed lady who played the piano and had a lovely singing voice. She was active and hard-working. When she stayed home to have children, she taught herself to be a cobbler so she could make her children's shoes.

Manya's father Wladislaw Sklodowski was a scholar who taught math and physics. He was a strong Polish nationalist. In 1830, his father had been captured in a revolt and was forced to march barefoot for 140 miles.

Years later in 1863, Manya's uncles fought in another revolt. The leaders of this revolt were hanged by Russian officials, and their bodies were left hanging all summer to decay. This was to scare any other Polish people from revolting, and the spot was only a few blocks from the Sklodowski home.

It is no surprise that Manya's father decided to take a different route to rebellion! He secretly taught his students about Polish scientists. At home on Saturday evenings, he recited Polish poetry to his children.

Manya's parents had five children. Sofia, nicknamed Zosia, was the eldest and acted like another mother to Manya. She would tell fairytales and perform plays for the family. Jozef was the only boy. Bronislawa (Bronya), and Helena came next. Finally, there was Manya. All of the children were talented and smart, but Manya was the brightest of all.

At the age of four, Manya took a book away from Bronya, who was struggling to read. She read a passage aloud without making any mistakes! Everyone was so surprised that Manya thought she had misbehaved and cried, "I didn't mean to do it, but it was so easy." By the time Manya was six and a half years old, she was already in the third grade. She even helped her older siblings with their school work.

The five siblings in 1872. From left to right: Zosia, Bronya, Manya, Jozef, and Helena.

In some ways, Manya grew up in two worlds. Her family was noisy and encouraged her to worry about her schoolwork less. Her siblings played war and built blocks with her. Manya's mother would affectionately run her fingers over Manya's forehead and encouraged her daughter to play more and read less.

The Sklodowskis had a brown dog named Lancet that Manya loved. Lancet was spoiled and the children gave him lots of treats. He jumped up on

The children's dog, Lancet, was a big pointer dog and beloved member of the family.

guests, knocked over vases of flowers with his tail, and ate everything he found.

Warsaw was a pretty town. In May, the lilac trees bloomed and fragranced the air. The older section of Warsaw had sculptures of religious saints and animals. In autumn, the leaves turned yellow and red along the nearby Vistula River. Apples were delivered from southern Poland, and Manya and her siblings filled their baskets with apples. They had fun tossing the rotten ones into the river.

But Manya lived in another world, too, both inside and outside the home. She had many fears including illness, death, the Russians, and school inspectors. She had good reason for these fears.

Manya and her siblings competed to see who could throw the rotten apples the farthest.

When Manya was four years old, her mother

developed tuberculosis. The children could hear her coughing and breathing painfully as she made their shoes in another room. Manya's mother never hugged or kissed her after that. She was too afraid of making her daughter sick.

Manya's father was fired from his teaching position because of his Polish nationalism. The family moved to a smaller house, and Wladislaw tutored up to twenty boys in the house. Many of them lived with the family in already cramped quarters. It was so noisy that Manya would stick her thumbs in her ears so she could concentrate on her reading. She read everything she could from poetry to her father's science journals.

At school Manya was the youngest, smallest, and shyest in her class. She wrote "I always wanted to run away and hide." She received top grades even though the schools were carefully watched by the Russians. If any Russian official caught a child speaking Polish, the whole class would be punished. So, Manya learned to speak Russian.

Secretly, her teacher, Madame Sikorska, taught the students Polish history and literature. A system was set up so that a bell would ring when a Russian school inspector was coming. When it did, the children would quickly hide any Polish books and papers, and begin speaking Russian.

Manya would later write that she would never forget the day that she had to stand in front of the class to answer the Russian school inspector's questions.

One day, Mr. Hornberg, the Russian school inspector, arrived. The twenty-five girls barely had enough time to hide their Polish papers. Mr. Hornberg wanted Madame Sikorska to choose a student to be interviewed (drilled, really) on their Russian lessons. Madame Sikorska chose Manya. Timid little Manya with her curly hair and navy blue uniform had to stand in front of the class and answer all of Mr. Hornberg's questions.

Tzar Alexander II was loved by the Russians but hated by the Poles

She answered each question perfectly.

At the end, Mr. Hornberg looked Manya straight in the eye and demanded, "Who is our beloved Tzar?" The Tzar was the leader of Russia, and all the Polish children hated him.

"Tzar Alexander II," she said.

Satisfied, Mr. Hornberg left the room. Manya felt like a traitor and burst into tears. The Russians had taken away the rights of the Polish people, but they could not change their hearts. Madame Sikorska gave Manya a hug and reassured her that she had done well.

In 1874, something terrible happened at home. One of the male students entered the house with typhus, a contagious disease contracted from lice, rats, and fleas. Bronya and Zosia contracted typhus. Bronya recovered in twelve days. After two weeks, Manya's funny and sweet eldest sister, Zosia, died. She was fourteen years old.

It was a cold day for Zosia's funeral. Manya's mother was very sick with tuberculosis. She watched the funeral procession from the window. She did not want eight-year-old Manya to catch cold, so she put her in Zosia's winter coat for the funeral.

Afterward, Manya spent months crying and hiding in small spaces. She did not know how to deal with the loss. Two years later, her mother died of tuberculosis. At the age of ten, Manya lost herself in books to keep from thinking of her mother.

Many people died of tuberculosis around the time that Zosia died. Sometimes, funeral processions would include multiple people and families.

CHAPTER TWO

Russian Control

Life went on. On her way to school each morning, Manya met up with her best friend Kazia. Manya continued to excel in school. She did not develop her mother's love for music, perhaps because it reminded her too painfully of her mother. Instead, she acquired her father's love of science. She dreamed of becoming a scientist.

Russian rule continued. In 1881, the Russian Tzar Alexander II was assassinated by a terrorist bomb. When Manya found out, she and her friends danced in the classroom.

One day, her friend Leonie Kunicka came to school upset. Her brother was sentenced to hang for plotting against the Russians. That night, Manya and four other girls went to Leonie's house. They stayed with Leonie when her brother died.

Manya's hard work in school paid off when she graduated first in her class, but it also left her stressed and worn out.

Manya knew any plots against the Russians could lead to death. There were spies who reported on people caught speaking Polish. But she knew that the fear inspired by the Russians also made the Poles more patriotic.

On the way to school, Manya and Kazia passed a statue that had been erected by the Russians. The statue was of Polish people who had made friends with the Russians. It was meant to show how Poles might be honored for such good behavior. Proud Poles considered such people to be traitors.

Manya later wrote: "All instruction was given in Russian, by the Russian professors, who . . . treated their pupils as enemies." By high school, Manya had learned to speak French, German, and English, in addition to Polish and Russian. She did not allow anything to keep her from her education.

In 1883 when Manya was sixteen years old, she graduated high school at the top of her class. She

Visiting the Carpathian Mountains in Southern Poland brought Manya fresh air and a newfound freedom away from Russian rule.

received the same gold medal that her brother Jozef and sister Bronya had once received.

By this time, Manya was exhausted. Her father decided that she needed a rest. He sent her to live with her uncles. She traveled through the countryside in southern Poland for an entire year. These uncles lived in the parts of Poland controlled by the Austrians. The Austrians were not as harsh as the Russians.

"There we could speak Polish in all freedom and sing patriotic songs without going to prison."

Manya brought her dog with her and developed a love of nature. She rolled hoops, climbed trees, made mud cakes, and played hide and seek with her cousins. She gathered fresh strawberries, gooseberries, and cherries. She went swimming, boating, fishing, and horseback riding.

In more quiet hours, she read, sketched, and listened to music. She was enchanted by the

At Christmas time in the country, families traveled by sleigh from one home to the next celebrating with their neighbors and friends.

Carpathian Mountains. She later wrote: "All my life through, the new sights of nature made me rejoice like a child."

In the winter, Manya took sleigh rides and attended festivals at neighbors' homes where there was plenty of food, music, and dancing. She and her cousins would eat all the pastries set out for the guests and escape outside to play before her aunts could catch them. In a childhood that had often been marked with fear and sorrow, Manya finally felt happy and free.

CHAPTER THREE

Education

When Manya returned home, she was a refreshed young woman. She had missed her father and her sister, Bronya. Bronya was practical, motherly, and intelligent. Bronya wanted to study medicine, and Manya wanted to study science.

However, in Poland women were not allowed to attend universities. For a while, a secret Polish university enrolled 200 women. However, when the Russians discovered it, the teachers were arrested and exiled.

The secret classes were taught by Polish scientists, philosophers, and historians at night and at different homes. The students then created a "floating," or "flying," university.

Risking imprisonment, Manya and Bronya attended classes in anatomy, natural history, and sociology.

Manya (left) and Bronya (right) posed for a photo in 1886. The two sisters were very devoted to each other.

The Sorbonne, a university in Paris, France, allowed female students. By the time Manya was seventeen and Bronya was twenty, Bronya could pay for one year at the Sorbonne.

There was not enough money for them both, but Manya had a plan. She told her sister that she would work as a governess in order to put Bronya through medical school. Once Bronya was a successful doctor, she would help put Manya through school.

Bronya left for Paris, and Manya got a job in town working as a governess. She did not like it, and it did not pay well. At the age of 18, Manya made the nerve-wracking decision to leave her father. She took a governess position in the agricultural town of Szczuki. It was a three-hour train ride and another four hours by sleigh for Manya to get there!

Manya lived with the Zorawski family. The property had a 200-acre beet farm and a beet factory. Mr. Zorawski was in charge of the peasants who worked on the farm and in the factory.

She taught the Zorawski's two daughters. Andzia was ten years old, and Bronka was Manya's age. Manya's salary was much better and the Zorawskis were nice.

When not teaching, Manya studied math and physics, but Manya wanted to do more. With permission from Mr. and Mrs. Zorawski, Manya and Bronka Zorawski taught the local children who did not go to school. They taught the children

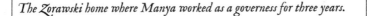
The Zorawski home where Manya worked as a governess for three years.

how to read and write in Polish even though it was "forbidden by the government and might bring imprisonment or deportation to Siberia."

Manya spent two to five hours per day teaching up to twenty peasant children. She used her own money to buy notebooks and pens for the children of servants, farmers, and factory workers. Many of the parents were illiterate and had little or no education. Sometimes they would stay in the back of the room to learn, too. Manya believed that, "You cannot hope to build a better world without improving the individuals."

Manya wrote letters to her family. Since she had no teacher, her father often sent her math problems. She was now a woman with gray eyes and a petite frame.

When the Zorawski's older son Casimir came home for a visit, he fell in love with Manya. The two planned a future together, but when Casimir told his parents, they were outraged. As nice as they had been to Manya, they did not want their son to marry a poor governess. Casimir broke off the engagement.

Manya was heartbroken, but she had not been fired, and the job paid well. So, Manya kept her

Upon visiting his parents, Casimir Zorawski did not expect to fall in love with his sisters' young governess.

promise to her sister and continued working for the Zorawskis for another year. In a letter she sent home in 1888, she wrote, "First principle: never to let one's self be beat down by persons or events." Still, it was a miserable, depressing year for her.

Finally, Manya's father found a teaching job that would help pay for both girls' education. Manya returned home. She took a nearby governess position and once again took secret classes. Her cousin, Joseph, gave Manya access to a laboratory. There she acquired a love for physics and chemistry experiments.

Soon, Bronya married a Polish doctor named Casimir Dluski, graduated with a medical degree, and invited Manya to come to Paris. Manya was still heartbroken over the breakup with her own Casimir Zorawski. She began to doubt whether she was meant to have a university education. This was when she wrote to Bronya telling her "I am stupid, and I shall remain stupid...[!]"

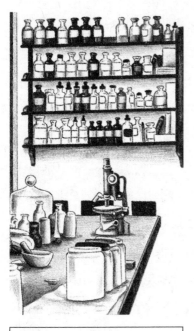

Manya's cousin was the director of the Museum of Industry and Agriculture which also served to secretly teach Polish students.

Bronya would not let her sister throw away a promising future. She convinced Manya to come to Paris and take classes at the Sorbonne. Eight years after Manya had graduated first-place in her high school, she was finally going to college.

In 1891, at 24 years old, she bought a train ticket to Paris. The trip took several days. Her fourth-class ticket required Manya to bring her own chair to sit on. Manya also brought a trunk of clothing and a feather mattress with her.

When Manya stepped off the train, she was surrounded by shops, crowds, and dust in the street. She was amazed. France was the art capital of Europe in the late 1800s. There was impressionist art from Degas, Monet, and Van Gogh. There were writers and dancers.

The Eiffel Tower was new and the tallest structure in the world. Paris had gaslights, telephones, and moving pictures. There was free speech! "It was like a new world opened to me," she wrote.

Manya moved in with Bronya and Casimir, who ran a medical practice together from their home. When she enrolled for physics classes at the

The Eiffel Tower was part of the International Exhibition of Paris in 1889. At the time, it was the tallest structure in the world at over 1,000 feet tall.

Sorbonne, she changed her name. By birth, her name was Maria, but now it would be Marie. Marie sounded more French, and she wanted to fit in.

The Sorbonne, or University of Paris, has a rich history that dates back to the 1200s.

Initially, Marie embraced both her academic and social life. But within her first year at the Sorbonne, Marie realized she had a problem. All her classes were now in French and she was having trouble keeping up.

In addition, her sister's house was noisy and distracting. Sick patients walked in and out of the home and medical practice at all hours. Living with Bronya was free, but it was also an hour from the Sorbonne. Traveling back and forth to school cut into Marie's study time, and she had to pay a bus fare, which was getting expensive. Marie needed to move.

With the few things she owned, Marie moved into the attic room on the sixth floor of a very run-down apartment building. Her room had no heating, lighting, running water, or elevator, but it was close to the Sorbonne.

Because her room was so cold, she would study in the school library until it closed at 10 p.m. each night. Then she would make her way up six flights of stairs to study by lamplight in her apartment until two in the morning. If she had a guest over, her old brown trunk doubled as an extra chair.

The water in her basin would sometimes freeze overnight. She piled all of her clothes on top of her blanket to keep warm. Food was another problem. Marie was not only poor, but she was so focused on her studies that she didn't want to take the time to eat. Her meals were nothing but some bread, an egg or a piece of fruit, and a cup of hot chocolate. She cooked the eggs over her alcohol lamp.

She would live like this for nearly three years. With so little sleep and food, Marie sometimes had fainting spells. Her brother-in-law heard from a friend about her living conditions and went to visit her. When he saw how weak she was, he brought her home to Bronya for rest and loving care. Bronya made sure Marie ate well, but as soon as Marie returned to her apartment, she went back to her old habits.

Marie was happy to focus on her education. Out of 2,000 students enrolled at the Sorbonne, there were only 23 women. In 1893, she became the first woman to receive a master's degree in physics at the Sorbonne.

She finished first in her class. She received the Alexandrovitch Scholarship for Polish students studying abroad, which allowed her to pursue a second degree. One year later, she received her master's degree in math, but was annoyed with herself for finishing in second place!

While getting her second degree, Marie was hired by the Society for the Encouragement of Natural Industry. They wanted her to research the magnetic properties of steel. Marie worked in the lab of Professor Gabriel Lippman.

Marie needed a bigger lab to do her research.

Marie's former professor Gabriel Lippman won a 1908 Nobel Prize in physics for advancing the technology of color photography.

She mentioned this need to a friend named Joseph Kowalski, who said he might know someone who could help Marie.

Marie's life was about to change forever.

CHAPTER FOUR

Pierre Curie

It was early 1894 when Joseph Kowalski, Marie Sklodowska, and Pierre Curie met for tea. For Pierre and Marie, there was instant chemistry.

Thirty years after they first met, Marie would describe Pierre as "a tall young man with auburn hair and large limpid eyes. I noticed the grave and gentle expression of his face, as well as a certain detachment in his attitude, suggesting the dreamer absorbed in his reflections."

When Pierre met Marie, he quickly fell in love.

Pierre was close to his brother Jacques (top left) and his parents. His parents homeschooled him when he was young because he had such a precocious mind.

Like Marie, Pierre was brilliant. He received a bachelor's degree by the age of sixteen and a Master's degree in physics by the time he was eighteen years old. He had a devoted mother, an intellectual father, and an older brother, Jacques, who was his best friend. Pierre and Jacques worked together in the lab.

In 1880, when Pierre was only twenty one years old, the brothers discovered piezoelectricity by studying quartz crystals. Today, piezoelectricity is used in sonar, ultrasound, cell phones, televisions, electric appliances, and quartz watches.

The brothers created an improved electrometer called a piezoelectric quartz electrometer. They also formulated a mathematical principle of symmetry known as "Curie's Law."

When Pierre met Marie, he was a thirty-five-year-old professor at the school of Physics and Chemistry and Marie was twenty six years old. Unfortunately, Pierre had no lab to offer Marie. However, he had finally found someone who could understand him. With their immediate attraction and shared love of science, they soon began dating. Pierre was able to locate a storage shed that Marie could use for her lab work.

In Pierre, Marie saw an honest man who enjoyed nature, painting, music, and scientific research. He was a gentle person who could become set on his decisions but was never angry. His father called him "the gentle stubborn one."

In spite of her affection for Pierre, Marie had always planned to return to her father in Poland. She wanted to continue helping the oppressed Polish people. When Pierre asked Marie to marry him, she turned him down. She had received two degrees at the Sorbonne and felt it was time to return to Poland.

Marie returned home, but "the gentle stubborn one" did not give up so easily. He wrote her letters to convince her to return to Paris. When that didn't work, he told her that he was willing to move to Poland.

Marie could see how serious Pierre was, and she loved him, too. Marie did not want to break her promise to her father, but she finally decided to return to Paris after her brother, Jozef, wrote her a letter. He told her to follow her heart without any regrets.

On July 26, 1895, Pierre and Marie Curie were married in a small city hall in the town where Pierre had been living with his parents. It was a tiny wedding with Pierre's family, Marie's father, her sisters Helena and Bronya, and Bronya's husband Casimir.

Of the marriage, Marie wrote: "So I had the privilege of entering into a family worthy of affection

Pierre and Marie both shared a love of nature and frugality, so biking across the French countryside was the perfect honeymoon!

and esteem, and where I found the warmest welcome."

Ever the practical and frugal scientists, the couple did not exchange wedding rings. Marie wore a dark dress that she could continue to use in her lab.

They took some money that had been given to them as a wedding gift and purchased two bicycles. They spent their month-long honeymoon bike riding through the French countryside. At night, they would find a nearby inn.

One lunchtime, Marie was resting on the moss near a pond. Her eyes were closed when Pierre dropped a frog into her hand. He thought it was interesting!

When their honeymoon ended, they returned to their lab work. In 1897, Marie completed her steel magnetism work and was paid for it.

She used the money to repay the scholarship money she had once received to continue her education at the Sorbonne. She was not obligated

Pierre's favorite picture of Marie was one he called "The Good Little Student."

to pay back this money, but she felt a strong desire to make sure there was enough money for another Polish student studying abroad.

Pierre encouraged Marie to continue to study and work towards a PhD. Pierre kept a picture of Marie in his pocket that he called "the good little student." It showed her with her hair up, wearing a striped blouse and looking off to the side.

Marie continued her studies while she was pregnant with their first child. She was dizzy and tired throughout the pregnancy, but continued her lab work and continued to take bike rides with Pierre. She gave birth to their first daughter Irène on September 12, 1897.

For her PhD thesis, Marie had chosen to study uranium rays, which had been discovered by Dr. Becquerel. This required lab work, which she loved. A short time later, Pierre's father Eugene came to live with Pierre and Marie. Pierre's mother had died of cancer a few weeks after Irène's birth.

A widower and retired doctor, Eugene was happy to stay home with baby Irène while Marie continued her research. Irène and her grandfather would develop a strong and loving relationship, and Marie's hard work in the lab would lead to an incredible discovery.

CHAPTER FIVE

Discovery!

In 1898, Marie's long hours in the lab were only just beginning. Thanks to Henri Becquerel, rays were known at the time, but no one knew how they worked. Marie wanted to find out. The small storage room that she used for a lab was as cold as forty-three degrees that February, but Marie had worked in cold conditions before.

She began testing Becquerel's uranium rays. She was convinced radiation came from uranium atoms and wondered what else might act that way. At the time, scientists believed that atoms could not change, but Marie questioned this theory.

In order to do this, she used Pierre's electrometer and piezoelectric quartz. With the electrometer she found that the element thorium also gave off rays.

She realized that the rays were actually the atoms giving off tiny particles. Atoms could change. Marie was the first to call these rays radiation and invent the word "radioactivity."

Marie worked with a substance called pitchblende in her lab. It was a black-brown mineral that was discarded as a by-product, or leftover, in uranium

In a cold, dingy, old shed, Marie discovered radioactivity. She was excited about the idea of discovering a new element!

mines. It contained uranium, thorium, and lead, was inexpensive, and was ideal for Marie to study.

Marie discovered that the pitchblende gave off much more radiation than uranium and thorium combined. Marie wondered if there was another element—an undiscovered element!—hidden in the pitchblende.

When Marie was born in 1867, only 63 elements in the world had been discovered (today there are 118 known elements). Was it possible that Marie was about to discover another element? This kind

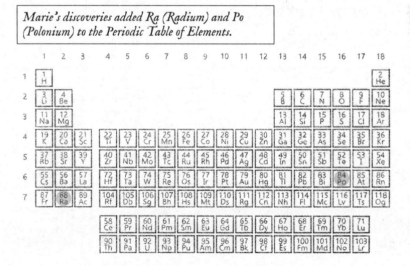

Marie's discoveries added Ra (Radium) and Po (Polonium) to the Periodic Table of Elements.

of research and testing would be time-consuming. It was such an incredible discovery, that Pierre decided to stop doing research on crystals in order to help his wife. Having worked closely for years with his brother, the idea of collaborating with Marie came naturally to Pierre.

Marie discovered not one, but two, new elements in 1898. She named the first one polonium after her beloved Poland. The second one she called radium, which is Latin for "ray." In order to prove these elements existed, they had to isolate, or pull them out of, the pitchblende. That would be the tricky part.

The Curies received no funding for their research and used their own money. They needed a bigger shed, more pitchblende, and more money. Pierre found a job at the Sorbonne in addition to working at the school of Physics and Chemistry.

Marie took a position as a physics professor at an elite school for young women. She was the only female teacher at the school, and it was more than an hour away from their home, but they needed money for their research.

Fortunately, they were able to get access to a larger shed. It had a leaky glass roof and was formerly used by medical students for dissecting dead bodies. An Austrian uranium mine donated pitchblende. The Curies only had to pay for the transportation of the pitchblende from the mine to

For a photo shoot in 1898, Pierre and Marie returned to the lab where they discovered two radioactive elements.

their shed. The piles of pitchblende, which looked like brown dirt mixed with pine needles, were delivered to the courtyard outside of the shed.

Separating the elements required boiling the pitchblende in water, acid, and other chemicals. The pitchblende smelled horrible, and Marie used a heavy iron rod nearly as big as herself to stir the mixture for hours at a time.

The cast iron pot held forty-four pounds (twenty kilograms) of pitchblende. There were many chemical treatments and careful notes with minute calculations taken. The shed was hot in summer, cold in winter, and wet when it rained.

This was how Marie described the experience: "Yet it was in this miserable old shed that we passed the best and happiest years of our life, devoting our entire days to our work. I would be broken with fatigue at the days' end."

She was able to separate out the polonium first. Radium would prove to be much trickier. In fact, they found that radium made up only one millionth of 1% of the pitchblende material. After boiling and treating tons of pitchblende, the Curies were able to produce 1/50 of a teaspoon of radium, or, the equivalent of a few grains of sand!

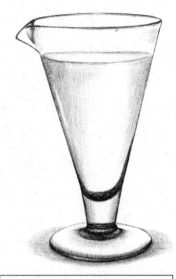

More than 100 years after Marie's discoveries, her notebooks, clothes, and lab equipment, like this flask, still contain dangerous levels of radioactivity.

It had taken them nearly four years after announcing the existence of radium to obtain 1/10 of a gram of radium in the form of salt. This was pure enough to be able to measure the atomic weight of of radium. On March 28, 1902, they proved that it was an undiscovered element.

Marie had always hoped that, when they isolated radium, it would be beautiful. She was not disappointed. Radium gave off a blue-green glow, and the Curies would sit at night gazing at their glorious radium.

"One of our joys was to go into our workroom at night; we then perceived on all sides the feebly luminous silhouettes of the bottles or capsules containing our products. . . . The glowing tubes looked like faint, fairy lights."

What they did not know was that, as they were boiling down the pitchblende and getting closer and closer to purified radium, the dangers of these "fairy lights" were growing.

In fact, it was the radioactive atoms releasing energy that was causing the radium to glow. The energy released by the radium made enough heat in one hour to melt then boil the equivalent weight of ice.

Pierre was taking notes that Marie was losing weight, he was experiencing terrible pains in his legs, and both of them had hard, painful fingertips and flu-like symptoms. They attributed some of this to hard work, not wanting to think that their life's work was causing such harm.

More than the discovery of two new elements, Marie had achieved a new method of discovering elements by measuring their radioactivity. In addition to using chemical methods, Marie used Pierre's delicate electrical equipment in order to examine radioactivity. This method has since led to the discovery of other radioactive elements.

Marie discovered that the radiation in radium was two million times stronger than uranium. The half-life of radium is 1600 years. That means it takes that many years for radium to lose half of its radioactivity. Furthermore, radium naturally produced a gas, or emanation, of radium along with producing heat.

The Curies decided not to get patents on radium, but rather chose to freely share their scientific knowledge. They wanted to help humanity rather than make money from their discoveries. Their generosity allowed the study of radioactivity to spread quickly, and they shared samples of radium with other important scientists.

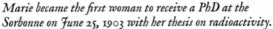

Marie became the first woman to receive a PhD at the Sorbonne on June 25, 1903 with her thesis on radioactivity.

As early as 1900, scientists Otto Walkhoof and Friedrich Giesel found that radium created changes in the body. Pierre studied this by taping radium salt to his lower arm for ten hours. It became a burn that turned into a deep wound with dead tissue around it.

Pierre's mother had died of breast cancer, and Pierre wondered if radium could be used in treating cancerous tissue. The Curies took emanations of radium and gave vials of it to doctors to use in cancer therapy. Doctors began testing radium on tumors and cancer cells, calling it "curietherapy."

This was the beginning of the radium industry. Marie's life was certainly getting exciting, but was also tinged with sadness. In 1902, her seventy-year-old father died.

Bronya moved with her husband back to Poland to open a tuberculosis hospital. Marie no longer had another relative in France. Marie also became pregnant again, but her baby died before birth.

Marie wrote to Bronya expressing her grief over the loss.

Through it all, Marie never stopped working. On June 25, 1903, Marie received her doctorate (PhD) degree from the Sorbonne. She was the first woman to ever receive a PhD in France. She did not sit back and rest after this achievement. For Marie Curie, the dedicated scientist, there was always more work to do. There were also more honors and recognition yet to come.

CHAPTER SIX

Nobel Prizes

Women at the time seldom had college educations, and wives were not expected to work outside the home. In fact, women were not taken seriously in the scientific community. Female scientists were at risk for having their discoveries stolen or credited to a male scientist.

Marie, however, was not shy about publishing papers under her own name. The Curies had a special relationship. Pierre saw Marie as his equal. He encouraged her passion for science. His father, too, helped out by being a nanny for baby Irène.

In 1896, Alfred Nobel, a Swedish chemist, inventor, engineer, and businessman died, leaving behind 355 patents and a vast fortune. While known for inventing dynamite, he was a pacifist.

He wanted his fortune to be used for a greater good. Upon his death, his will established the Nobel Prize, one of the most prestigious awards that anyone can earn. The Nobel Prize is given each year in physics, chemistry, physiology or medicine, literature, and peace. The first Nobel Prize was given

Alfred Nobel died in 1896 and left today's equivalent of $265 million in his will to fund annual Nobel prizes.

in 1901 to Wilhelm Conrad Rontgen in physics. He discovered the x-ray.

In 1903, a Nobel committee member wrote to Pierre. Pierre and Becquerel, the man who discovered the Becquerel rays in uranium, had been nominated for a Nobel Prize in physics for their research on radiation. Marie was not mentioned.

Pierre politely wrote back: "If it is true that one is seriously thinking about me, I very much wish to be considered together with Madame Curie with respect to our research on radioactive bodies."

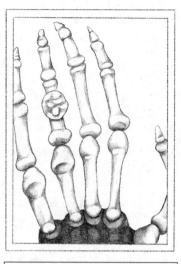

Wilhelm Conrad Rontgen took the first x-ray. It was of his wife's hand along with the ring on her finger.

As a result, Marie was allowed to share the prize with her husband. Becquerel received half, and the Curies shared the other half as if they were one person.

Part of the honor of winning a Nobel Prize included giving a speech in Stockholm, Sweden. However, Marie was too ill to attend the award ceremony. They traveled to Sweden sixteen months later. Pierre gave the speech while Marie sat in the audience.

Marie's happiest hours were spent in the lab. She and Pierre were annoyed by the distractions that came with being famous.

It was a great honor and a huge fortune to the Curies. The prize money amounted to about $20,000, which would be worth about a half-million dollars today.

They gave generously to their family and friends. Marie even gave a teacher back in Poland money to visit her French relatives.

The Curies did not spend much on themselves. They felt they had splurged when they built a modern bathroom in their home! They used some of the money to hire a lab assistant. The Sorbonne hired Pierre as a physics professor, and he made Marie his laboratory chief.

Pierre and Marie were very private, busy scientists. Now everyone knew who they were. They received letters along with unexpected visitors and many reporters. Marie wrote to her brother Jozef: "...our life has been altogether spoiled by honors and fame."

When they went on trips, they used fake names, or pseudonyms, so that reporters wouldn't find them. Reporters even wrote about Didi, the Curie's black and white cat!

On December 6, 1904, Marie gave birth to a second daughter Ève. The sisters were very different from each other. Seven-year-old Irène had light hair and green-brown eyes, whereas Ève had dark hair and blue eyes. Irène would later show an interest in science like her mother, but Ève would be interested in music like Marie's mother had once been.

At Easter time in April of 1906, the Curies took Irène and toddler Ève to the countryside for a vacation. Marie always loved having flowers in the house, and Pierre picked a fresh bouquet of water buttercups. After a while, he became restless and decided to return home before Marie and the girls. He took the flowers home with him.

Once home, Pierre had meetings to attend. April 19, 1906 was a rainy, dismal day in Paris, and Pierre carried his black umbrella with him. By this time, his work with radium was causing such pain in his legs that he limped.

Pierre was lost in thought as he walked the wet streets that were filled with people and horse-drawn carriages. At that moment, two large plow-horses were pulling a twenty-foot long, six-ton cart full of military uniforms.

As Pierre stepped into the street, he saw the cart at the last second. He tried to grab onto the horse's bridle, but fell. The front two wheels of the cart just missed Pierre. The rear wheel did not.

The busy streets of Paris were dangerous on a clear day, but even more so in bad weather.

Pierre Curie—husband, father, and renowned scientist—was dead at the age of forty-six. His skull had been crushed. Someone attempted to get a cab driver to put Pierre in a carriage, but the cab drivers did not want blood in their cab.

When the crowd recognized Pierre, they turned violent against the cart driver. He was saved by the police. The police brought Pierre's body to the police station on a stretcher, where a lab assistant identified him.

Marie and the girls were still on vacation, so the news came first to Pierre's father, Eugene. Upon hearing the news, Eugene simply said, "My son is dead. . . . What was he dreaming of this time?"

When Marie came home, she was eager to see Pierre and return to her research. What she was not expecting was to be met at the house by her close friends. They looked somber.

When they told her what happened, she was in disbelief. The water buttercups were still fresh in

Marie, Irène, and Ève posed together in 1908.

Marie found it hard to believe that the flowers would continue to live while her husband was gone. It took a long time for her to enjoy fresh flowers again.

the vase. She said to her friends, "Pierre is dead. Dead. Absolutely dead?"

As with the loss of her sister and mother years earlier, Pierre's death sent Marie into a depression. A neighbor cared for the girls while Marie took to her bed. On April 30, 1906 Marie wrote to Pierre in a journal: "I live only for your memory and to make you proud of me."

Separating her emotions from her scientific research, Marie continued her work.

She took her daughters and moved to Sceaux, where Pierre had grown up and where he was buried. She wanted to be close to Pierre and away from their Paris home.

She was offered a pension from the Sorbonne but turned it down. Marie thought she was too young to accept a pension and decided she would support her children herself. But how?

Fortunately, the Sorbonne unanimously voted to give her Pierre's old position. Marie would teach her first class on November 5, 1906, two days before her thirty-ninth birthday. She was the first female professor at the university.

Marie gave her first lecture at the Sorbonne to hundreds of people in attendance.

As she stood at the front of the lecture hall on that first day, hundreds of people came to watch. Everyone was curious about what she would say, if she would speak about Pierre, or if she would fail as a professor.

American millionaire Andrew Carnegie provided critical funds to Marie's laboratory, allowing her scientific research to continue at a steady pace.

Marie surprised everyone. She cleared her throat.

"When one considers the progress that has been made in physics in the past ten years, one is surprised at the advance that has taken place in our ideas concerning electricity and matter." Marie began her first lecture with the exact sentence where Pierre had left off with his last one.

Shortly after Pierre's death, Marie met the famous American millionaire Andrew Carnegie. Carnegie was a philanthropist and was impressed with Marie's work. He donated money for her to hire a research staff and plan a school on radioactivity.

The annual income that came from Carnegie allowed the students and scientists to devote more time to their lab work without having to take on second jobs.

In 1907, they found the atomic weight of radium, and by 1910, they successfully isolated the metal from other impurities. The Curie lab grew from eight to twenty-two employees between 1908 and 1910.

In addition, twenty women scientists volunteered in the lab without pay. Marie established the standard for radium emissions. Today, a unit of radioactivity is called a "curie."

Eugene Curie died in 1910, and Marie hired a Polish governess to care for the girls, aged thirteen and six. She also began a new experiment that year. Since her friends were all scientists, she organized a group of them to homeschool their collective ten children.

They took turns teaching Irène, Ève, and the other children one lecture per day on just one topic. For two years, the children were taught French, German, English, geography, history, natural science, math, physics, and chemistry. Marie taught chemistry in her laboratory. Irène's interest in science began to blossom.

Marie placed a high value on physical education, expecially for girls. Girls were seldom encouraged to be athletic at the time.

Marie also believed in physical education. "Next to outdoor walks, I attach a great importance to gymnastics and sports. This side of a girl's education is still rather neglected in France." The girls were very good at swimming, canoeing, and bicycle riding.

In 1911, on Marie's birthday, a telegram arrived. She was being awarded a second Nobel, the first person to ever receive two such awards. This Nobel was in chemistry for the discovery of radium and polonium.

Marie traveled to Sweden to give the acceptance speech. The trip left her exhausted, feverish, and with kidney pain. She needed a kidney operation, and her recovery took more than a year. During that time, she hardly saw her daughters and could not work.

In 1912, Marie traveled to Warsaw, Poland to give a speech. In the audience was Madame Sikorska, the teacher who had once comforted her when she was forced to answer the Russian inspector's questions. At the end of her speech, Marie gave Madame Sikorska a kiss. How proud her teacher must have been of Marie's achievements!

Marie's success came with the opportunity to meet other famous scientists. In 1913, Marie and Albert Einstein became friends. Einstein, his wife, and son even took a backpacking trip with Marie, Irène, and Ève. Einstein greatly respected Marie and discussed his theories with her.

The Sorbonne and Pasteur Institutes agreed to combine funds to create a radium institute. It would have a lab for radioactivity, and a lab for biology research and curietherapy to study cancer treatments.

The Institute was Marie's pride and joy and a way of honoring Pierre. She wanted it to be perfect and oversaw every detail of the institute, including the landscaping. Marie planted the climbing roses outside of her office herself. In July of 1914, the Institute was ready for its grand opening.

Unfortunately, war was about to break out.

In a speech in honor of Marie, Albert Einstein said, "It was my good fortune to be linked with Madame Curie through twenty years of sublime and unclouded friendship."

CHAPTER SEVEN

World War I

On August 3, 1914, Germany declared war on France. One month later, German soldiers invaded France, heading toward Paris. Marie sent her girls along with their Polish governess to the seacoast of Brittany while she stayed behind in Paris.

The Radium Institute would have to wait, for Marie had a very important job to do. She needed to keep the radium safely out of the hands of the Germans. Marie took the isolated radium and encased it in lead. She carried it in a suitcase for a 10-hour trip to Bordeaux, where it would be kept in a vault.

Bordeaux was where the French government had retreated. When she got there, the hotels were already overcrowded from people escaping Paris.

Her bag had become too heavy for her to carry. She found a government employee who was kind enough to find her a room in a private apartment and carry her bag for her.

As she was returning to Paris, the Battle of the Marne had begun. Thankfully, the British and French forces were able to stop the German advance and Paris was safe again. Marie soon brought Irène and Ève back home.

All of Marie's workers at the institute had joined the war effort. There was no one left to do the work. Marie did not believe in war, but she was very determined to help the war effort through peaceful means. She wrote to her friend Hertha Ayrton "Only through peaceful means can we achieve an ideal society."

Marie brought her Nobel money and her gold Nobel medals to buy war bonds. She wanted the medals to be melted down and used to help France win the war. The French official recognized Marie and refused to take her medals. She wanted to do more, but what?

Marie discovered that health services were in particular need during the war. Badly injured soldiers with missing limbs and nearly useless bodies were returning to Paris. Many of their injuries were made worse by doctors who probed their bodies searching for bullets.

Marie realized that x-ray machines could easily find the exact location of bullets inside bodies, giving the patients a much greater chance of recovery and survival. Not all hospitals had x-ray machines since only a few knowledgeable experts in the bigger hospitals knew how to use them.

To meet the demand of the injured soldiers, hospitals were springing up all over the country with no x-ray services available. The Military Board of Health did not have a radiologic branch.

Marie took action. She studied human anatomy. She learned how to use an x-ray machine. She borrowed x-ray machines from labs and doctors' offices which were not in use.

First she established radiology stations, creating or improving 200 radiological installations. Then she came up with a brilliant idea: mobile x-ray units.

Marie borrowed a car from the Red Cross and created a radiologic car. It could be driven directly

A "Little Curie," or mobile x-ray unit to transport the x-ray machines to the injured soldiers on the battlefield, could travel at speeds of about twenty miles per hour.

to the battlefields to x-ray soldiers before they were transported to hospitals. She realized how successful the mobile x-ray unit could be.

This was no easy task. For starters Marie had to learn how to drive! She obtained her driver's license, learned to turn the crank on the car motor, change a tire, and clean a carburetor.

She visited wealthy women and got them to donate their cars for the war effort. In this way she was able to create a total of twenty mobile military units which became known as "little curies."

These small cars were able to navigate narrow roads, and each unit had a small generator for when there was no electricity on-site. The x-ray machines had movable stands so they could be wheeled into place. A folding table for the patient and heavy curtains to keep out the light during the x-ray process were added.

Marie would drive to a field hospital, unload the equipment, and hook up the generator. Then she got out the table, covered the windows, and was ready to start the x-ray machine for the first soldier in line.

But Marie was only one person. Who else could drive and operate these little curies? The machines were useless if no one knew how to operate them. Marie had the answer to that, too.

At first, she found some professors, engineers, students, and soldiers not serving active duty at the

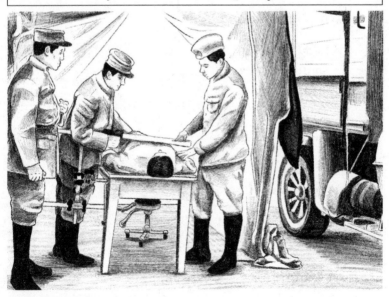

Trained radiological assistants could x-ray an injured soldier and determine exact bullet locations for doctors to remove more efficiently.

time. However, it took several days to train them, and eventually many of these people would get called to duty.

Marie realized the answer was to train women. She helped teach women how to take x-rays. For protection, they wore cotton gloves and a lead-filled apron. The little curies traveled through France and Belgium saving thousands of lives.

Marie chose seventeen-year-old Irène to be her first radiological assistant. The two women made their first trip to a battlefield in 1914.

By telephone or telegrams, they would get information about a battle and drive to the location to help. It took them only thirty minutes to set up the equipment. They did not stop working until every soldier who needed an x-ray had received one.

Irène was trained and eventually had her own little curie. Her mother left her in charge of a radiological facility in Belgium. Irène was left to x-ray soldiers and

Irène and Marie at a Belgium hospital with radiographic equipment in 1915.

create diagrams to show the doctors and surgeons the exact bullet locations.

Intellectually gifted with a strong work ethic like her mother, Irène attended the Sorbonne and simultaneously went to nursing school. She trained herself to repair the x-ray equipment and spent her eighteenth birthday training other nurses.

In 1915, Marie brought the radium she had hidden back to Paris. Meanwhile, she was still keeping an eye on her Radium Institute waiting for the end of the war. She donated vials of radium emanations to use in radium-therapy for wounded soldiers.

The emanations did not deplete the radium source, which Marie needed for the Institute. The emanations were a natural byproduct and Marie was happy to help.

In 1916, Marie asked the French Health Services to add a radiology department to a recently-opened nursing school. Irène helped teach a training course for women. Eventually, 150 women were trained. Irène graduated from the Sorbonne with honors in mathematics, physics, and chemistry.

The Board of Health created their own radiologic services after seeing the life-saving work of the Curies. Having trained x-ray technicians not only opened doors for women, but, by the end of World War I, one million soldiers had been x-rayed!

On November 11, 1918, after four long years, World War I came to an end. Twenty million people had died, and twenty-one million were wounded. Sixteen percent of France's young men had perished.

While the men were at war, the women had kept the country running. They took over factories, schools, farms, and hospitals. For her part, Marie had achieved her goal of serving peacefully.

That same year, the Radium Institute finally opened. It did not have nearly enough workers or equipment quite yet. Still, it was a dream come true for Marie.

It was not the only dream, however. In 1919 the Treaty of Versailles made Marie's beloved home country of Poland a free country after more than a century of foreign rule. In her 1929 book *Pierre Curie*, Marie wrote:

> "The dream that appeared so difficult to realize, although so dear, became a reality following the storm that swept over Europe."

The nurses knew that they were putting themselves at risk by exposing themselves to the x-rays, but it was worth it.

CHAPTER EIGHT

Radium in America

Marie was unhappy about the exploitation of radium, but she could not stop it. In 1916, the Radium Luminous Materials Corporation in East Orange, New Jersey made wristwatches that glowed in the dark.

They hired young women who painted the watch dials with radium paint. In order to make clear, easy to read numbers, they sharpened the paintbrush tip between their lips. By the end of the day, each woman had painted between 250–300 watch dials.

The women did not know they were working with poison. During breaks, they painted their teeth, hair, or clothing and went into a dark closet to see it glow.

By 1919, two million radium dials were produced. By this time, toxic radium was in their teeth, bones, and organs. Several women needed teeth pulled out. Once the decaying teeth were removed, the bone and flesh around them also rotted. The women suffered extreme fatigue. The first woman, Mollie Maggia, died in 1922. Doctors noticed that a mysterious disease was striking the dial painters.

Five brave young women decided to sue the U.S. Radium Corporation. The corporation claimed the illnesses had nothing to do with radium, but they lost the court battle.

The corporation gave each woman $10,000 ($150,000 now), $600 per year for life ($9,000 now), and paid their medical bills. This was a huge sum of money, but it could not save the "Radium Girls." Each of them slowly died.

Radithor was the deadliest of all the radium products. Radithor owner, William Bailey, called it "perpetual sunshine" and claimed it cured 68 different ailments. Each bottle cost $1, about $14.50 now. In the 1920's, 400,000 bottles were sold.

The millionaire Eben Byers, son of a wealthy American industrialist, loved Radithor. In 1927, he drank several bottles a day and gave bottles to his friends and even to his racehorses. By 1930, Eben's teeth fell out. By 1932, he was dead. The amount of radium in his body was the largest amount ever found in a human being.

Radithor was more dangerous than many other radium products on the market because the owner made sure that each bottle contained actual radium. He did not want to be accused of false advertising!

If all these people were dying from radium poisoning within a few years, why hadn't Marie Curie died after all her research? Unlike Eben Byers and the Radium Girls, Marie never ingested the radium.

That did not mean Marie experienced no side effects. She and Pierre had suffered numb fingers, exhaustion, and flu-like symptoms. Pierre's weakened legs probably contributed to his death.

Later on, Marie developed a constant humming in her ears and cataracts which left her nearly blind. She continued giving lectures by writing her notes in large letters. Marie's strong belief in exercise and fresh air may have helped her to stay strong.

In 1920, Marie was interviewed by an American reporter named Missy Meloney. Missy was the editor of *Delineator*, an American women's magazine. American women had gained the right to vote one year earlier.

Missy asked Marie why she did not have a fortune in patents. Marie responded, "There were no patents. We were working in the interests of science. Radium was not to enrich anyone. Radium is an element. It belongs to all people."

The gram of radium that she and Pierre had produced belonged to the Radium Institute. Marie needed more radium to continue her research. One gram of radium cost $100,000 at the time, $1.3 million now, and she could not afford it.

Missy asked her where radium could be found. "'America,' she said, 'has about fifty grams of radium. Four of these are in Baltimore, six in Denver, seven in New York.' She went on naming the location of every grain."

Missy and Marie became friends. Missy started a fundraiser in the United States with a news article titled "That Millions Shall Not Die." She wanted donations from American women so Marie could continue her research. One donor gave $10,000 ($133,000 now) because her cancer was cured with radium treatments.

Missy raised $150,000 (nearly $2 million now) and the Standard Chemical Company produced a gram of radium for Marie. Marie was in poor health and did not like to travel, but Missy promised to stay with her if she visited America.

Marie and her daughters arrived in the US in 1921. They were greeted by women, girl scouts, women's

From left to right, Missy, Irène, Marie, and Ève went to America in 1921. It was Marie's first time visiting the country.

college representatives, journalists, photographers, and US Polish organizations. In her honor, they flew the United States, Polish, and French flags. Within a few days, Marie's arm was in a sling from shaking so many hands!

Marie met United States President Warren G. Harding, who gave her a certificate stating that the radium was for the Radium Institute in France. He also gave her a gold key to unlock the box

Pierre Curie came out in 1923. Instead of writing her own autobiography, Marie decided to focus on the life of her husband. However, there are also autobiographical notes in the book.

of radium which had been stored for shipping. The extra fundraising money was for scientific equipment and research.

Missy convinced Marie to write a book and she found Marie a publisher in the United States. Marie wrote the book *Pierre Curie*. In it, she described her visit to America:

> "I got back to France with a feeling of gratitude for the precious gift of the American women, and with a feeling of affection for their great country tied with ours by a mutual sympathy which gives confidence in a peaceful future for humanity."

Back at home, Marie employed an ethnically diverse group of people, including women. Some of these scientists went on to achieve fame.

Ellen Gleditsch published articles and books on radioactivity and inorganic chemistry.

Eva Ramstedt was a Swedish physicist who later worked at the Nobel Institute.

Marguerite Perry discovered the element francium in 1939 at the Radium Institute. In 1962, Perry became the first female member of the French Academy of Science.

During Marie's life, the Academy of Science refused to admit women. However, the French Academy of Medicine elected Marie as their first female member. She also became the vice president of the International Committee on Intellectual Cooperation in the League of Nations.

After the French Radium Institute became successful, Marie created a second institute in Poland. Once again she needed money for radium. Missy Meloney started a second fundraiser in 1929.

Marie's Radium Institute was located in Paris, France.

On October 16, 1929 Marie made her second trip to America. By this time, radium prices had come down, and President Hoover presented her with $50,000.

If her campaign had come any later, she may have missed her opportunity. The initial 1929 Stock Market Crash occurred on October 24th, and America soon entered the Great Depression.

The Maria Sklodowska Curie Institute of Warsaw Poland opened in 1932. This would be Marie's last trip to her homeland. She was so proud of how far Poland had come from the days of her childhood.

Marie continued to oversee the work at the French Radium Institute. She went home early one day, feeling tired, but still noticed that the roses by her office needed tending.

On July 4, 1934 at the age of sixty-six, Marie Curie died from complications brought on by radium poisoning. She was buried next to her husband Pierre. Her siblings, Jozef and Bronya, scattered a handful of Polish dirt on her coffin along with roses.

In 1995, the French government moved the remains of Pierre and Marie to the Panthéon in Paris, were France's greatest people are put to rest. Almost six decades after her death, Marie accomplished another first: she was the first woman to be buried at the Panthéon for her own accomplishments.

Irène accepting an honorary degree at the University of Pennsylvania for her mother. Marie was too weak to attend all the festivities the Americans had planned during her 1921 US visit.

CHAPTER NINE

Her Legacy

Marie Curie was one of the most famous scientists in the world. Her study of radium began the Atomic (Nuclear) age. Nuclear energy today is used in power plants, submarines, and spaceships. Radiation treatment is used to treat cancer. Radioactive elements are used in medical equipment and other industries.

Marie received international fame and was welcomed by presidents, ambassadors, kings, and queens. Her and Pierre's faces appear on the 500 franc note (a collectors' item), and on stamps and coins. Marie was never interested in fame, but movies have been made about her.

Marie's daughters also achieved fame. Ève wrote her mother's biography, titled *Madame Curie*, a title by which Marie is often known. Ève joined the resistance as a World War II correspondent and married Henry Labouisse. He became the director of UNICEF (United Nations International Children's Emergency Fund), which won a Nobel Peace prize in 1965. Ève lived to 102 years old!

Irène followed in her mother's footsteps, marrying a scientist at the Radium Institute named

The bodies of Marie and Pierre Curie were placed in the Panthéon in Paris in 1995. Their remains were carefully dug up, but they did not contain dangerous levels of radioactivity.

Frédéric Joliot. Irène and Fred discovered artificial radioactivity. This allowed faster progress of nuclear physics and medicine, and the couple won the 1935 Nobel in chemistry.

A French coin marked "Marie Curie" is one of many ways in which Marie has been memorialized.

Irène became the second woman to receive a Nobel in chemistry. She also gave lectures and helped women's rights (France gave women the right to vote in 1945). Sadly, Irène died at the age of fifty-eight from leukemia, most likely from working with radiation.

Irène's daughter Hélène worked as a researcher for her father, and they created France's first atomic reactor, which was enabled in 1948.

Eventually, France would generate nearly eighty percent of its electricity through nuclear power. Hélène was a nuclear physics professor and her brother Pierre became a biochemistry professor.

Marie left us with a whole new world of science to explore, and her descendants have carried on the tradition. Her story can teach us much more. She was a woman who overcame poverty, humiliation, fear, depression, heartbreak, and profound grief. How did she do this? Marie had persistence, perseverance, tenacity, and endless curiosity. Marie Curie simply never gave up.

Today, nuclear power plants are used throughout the world, including France, the United States, Russia, China, and India.

Marie Sklodowska Curie statue in Warsaw faces the Polish Radium Institute that Marie established in 1932. Her sister Bronya became the director of the institute, which today is the leading cancer treatment center in Poland.

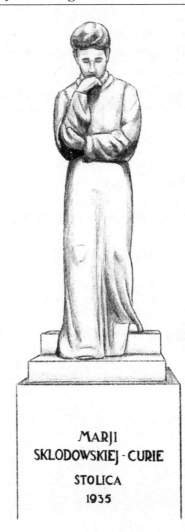

MARJI
SKLODOWSKIEJ - CURIE
STOLICA
1935

"Nothing in life is to be feared, it is only to be understood. Now is the time to understand more so that we may fear less."

"A scientist in his laboratory is not a mere technician: he is also a child confronting natural phenomena that impress him as though they were fairy tales."

"Be less curious about people and more curious about ideas."

"Life is not easy for any of us. But what of that? We must have perseverance and above all confidence in ourselves. We must believe that we are gifted for something and that this thing must be attained."

"I was taught that the way of progress was neither swift nor easy."

"One never notices what has been done; one can only see what remains to be done."

Claire Caprioli has written multiple nonfiction articles for award-winning children's magazines *Calliope and Faces*. She had an early career in technical writing and editing in information technology. She has always been interested in biographies and children's writing, but also spent fourteen years writing monthly parenting and pregnancy articles for a local midwifery newsletter and blogpost. Over the past decade she has been a tutor, aid, and cheerleader for various middle and high school-level Science Olympiad events.

Assassinate: To kill an important person in a surprise attack, usually for political or religious reasons.

Atom: The smallest part of an element that still has all the properties of that element. Atoms can only be seen with powerful microscopes.

Atomic weight: the mass of one atom of a chemical element. The measurements are in atomic mass units.

Artificial radioactivity: Man-made radioactivity which occurs when a stable material is exposed to radiation.

Brittany: A region northwest of France and southwest of Normandy.

By-product: A secondary product made in the manufacturing of something else.

Cancer: A group of more than 100 diseases that involve the uncontrolled growth of abnormal cells in the body.

Capture: The act of catching or gaining control, usually by force or trickery.

Chemistry: The science that deals with elements and compounds, their properties, composition, and structure, along with the energy they release.

Cobbler: A person who makes and/or mends shoes.

Curietherapy: Also known as radiotherapy, radium therapy, or radiation therapy, which is often a form of cancer treatment where the patient is exposed to radiation.

Electrometer: An instrument for measuring an electric charge, designed to measure very small voltages and currents. There are many different kinds of electrometers.

Element: A material that cannot be separated because it is pure.

Emanation: A discharge or product given off from its source.

Exiled: being forced to leave one's home or country.

Exploitation: Making use of a resource, often for a financial benefit.

Fragrance (v): To fill the air with a pleasant smell.

Flying/Floating University: The secret and illegal education system set up in Poland to give Polish people, especially women, a Polish university education during the time of Russian rule. It was "flying" because teachers and students moved classes from house to house to avoid being caught.

Frugality: To be careful with spending money or using resources.

Gaslights: A light fixture or streetlamp powered by burning gas.

Governess: A woman who takes care of and teaches children in their homes.

Half-life: The number of years it takes for a radioactive element to lose half of its radioactivity.

League of Nations: A political organization established at the end of World War I, later replaced by the United Nations.

Limpid: Perfectly clear.

Master's Degree: the first level of graduate study after receiving a bachelor's undergraduate (college) degree. This typically takes 1-2 years of study.

Mineral: A solid chemical compound that occurs naturally

Nationalist/ism: A person who is loyal, devoted, and patriotic to a nation/country often with a strong sense of political independence for the country.

Nobel Prize: An annual and prestigious award given in one of several categories. It is considered the highest intellectual achievement, and was created by the Swedish inventor and industrialist Alfred Nobel.

Oppressive: Causing undo hardship and cruel restrictions often on a minority or group.

Pacifist: A person who does not believe in war or violence for any reason.

Patent: The exclusive right to a new invention or process.

Patriotism: Support for one's country.

Pension: Regular payments made by a person's employer after (s)he has retired. It may be given to the spouse if the former employee has died.

Periodic Table of elements: An organized chart of all the chemical elements in order of increasing atomic number (which is the number of protons in the nucleus of an element).

Philanthropist: A person who helps others by giving generously to good causes.

Physics: Field of science that studies matter and energy and how they interact, such as with motion.

PhD: A doctorate degree is the highest degree given by a university in subjects other than medicine.

Piezoelectricity: Electric polarization in a material (such as certain crystals) from applying mechanical stress.

Pitchblende: A mixture of materials that contains uranium, polonium, and radium.

Pole: A Polish person.

Polonium: A radioactive element.

Precocious: To show the qualities or abilities of an adult at an unusually early age.

Prestigious: Distinguished and inspiring respect from others.

Radiation: A material that gives off powerful rays of energy, based on the Latin word for "ray."

Radium: a radioactive element that can be used in very small doses to treat cancer, but in larger doses can cause cancer and other illnesses.

Radioactive: Materials that give off radiation.

Radiation poisoning: Sickness resulting from excessive exposure to ionizing radiation, causing tissue damage and sometimes death.

Radiology/Radiological: Having to do with the science of x-rays and other high-energy radiation.

Rebel: Someone who fights against the government, ruler, or laws governing them.

Rebellion: An open opposition to authority, usually a government or ruler

Religious Saints: A holy person who is recognized by an official religion, usually Christian.

Revolt: To rise up against the authority of a ruler or government, similar to rebel

Sorbonne: The University of Paris in France from 1257 to 1970. As of 2018, Sorbonne University is a public research university in Paris, combining the Paris-Sorbonne University and the Pierre and Marie Curie University.

Telegram: A message sent by telegraph, an electric device to send messages by code over wire that predated the telephone.

Thesis: A long well-researched essay presented by a student in order to obtain a degree.

Thorium: A metallic element that has a weak amount of radioactivity.

Tuberculosis: A contagious disease that effects the lungs. It can be cured today with medication.

Typhus: A sudden and infectious disease lasting several weeks that causes headaches, chills, fever, pains, rash, and can lead to blood infection (toxemia) and death.

Uranium: An element that gives off radiation and makes atomic energy.

Vial: A small, cylindrical glass container often used for medicine.

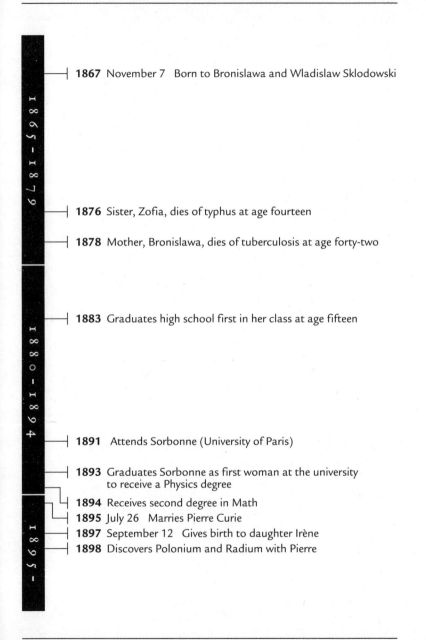

1867 November 7 Born to Bronislawa and Wladislaw Sklodowski

1865–1879

1876 Sister, Zofia, dies of typhus at age fourteen

1878 Mother, Bronislawa, dies of tuberculosis at age forty-two

1883 Graduates high school first in her class at age fifteen

1880–1894

1891 Attends Sorbonne (University of Paris)

1893 Graduates Sorbonne as first woman at the university to receive a Physics degree

1894 Receives second degree in Math

1895 July 26 Marries Pierre Curie

1897 September 12 Gives birth to daughter Irène

1898 Discovers Polonium and Radium with Pierre

1895–

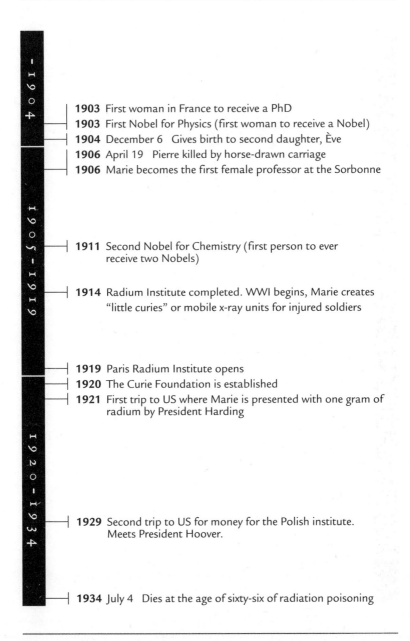

1903 First woman in France to receive a PhD
1903 First Nobel for Physics (first woman to receive a Nobel)
1904 December 6   Gives birth to second daughter, Ève
1906 April 19   Pierre killed by horse-drawn carriage
1906 Marie becomes the first female professor at the Sorbonne

1911 Second Nobel for Chemistry (first person to ever receive two Nobels)

1914 Radium Institute completed. WWI begins, Marie creates "little curies" or mobile x-ray units for injured soldiers

1919 Paris Radium Institute opens
1920 The Curie Foundation is established
1921 First trip to US where Marie is presented with one gram of radium by President Harding

1929 Second trip to US for money for the Polish institute. Meets President Hoover.

1934 July 4   Dies at the age of sixty-six of radiation poisoning

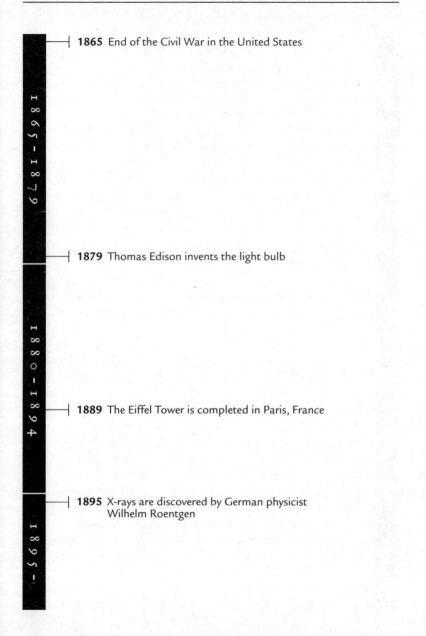

1865 End of the Civil War in the United States

1865 – 1879

1879 Thomas Edison invents the light bulb

1880 – 1894

1889 The Eiffel Tower is completed in Paris, France

1895 X-rays are discovered by German physicist
Wilhelm Roentgen

1895 –

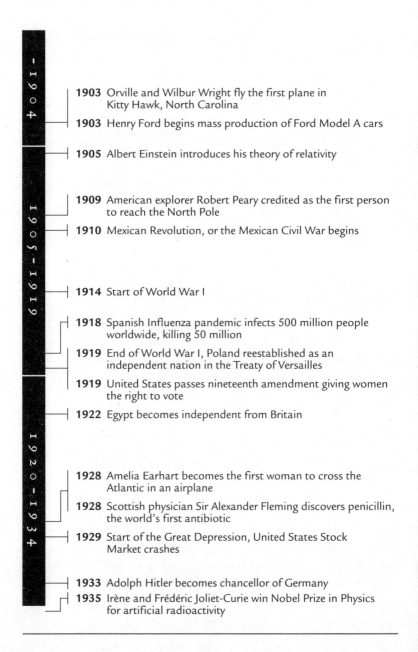

1904

1903 Orville and Wilbur Wright fly the first plane in Kitty Hawk, North Carolina

1903 Henry Ford begins mass production of Ford Model A cars

1905 Albert Einstein introduces his theory of relativity

1909 American explorer Robert Peary credited as the first person to reach the North Pole

1910 Mexican Revolution, or the Mexican Civil War begins

1905 - 1919

1914 Start of World War I

1918 Spanish Influenza pandemic infects 500 million people worldwide, killing 50 million

1919 End of World War I, Poland reestablished as an independent nation in the Treaty of Versailles

1919 United States passes nineteenth amendment giving women the right to vote

1922 Egypt becomes independent from Britain

1920 - 1934

1928 Amelia Earhart becomes the first woman to cross the Atlantic in an airplane

1928 Scottish physician Sir Alexander Fleming discovers penicillin, the world's first antibiotic

1929 Start of the Great Depression, United States Stock Market crashes

1933 Adolph Hitler becomes chancellor of Germany

1935 Irène and Frédéric Joliet-Curie win Nobel Prize in Physics for artificial radioactivity

Cullen, Katherine E. *Science, Technology, and Society: the People behind the Science.* Chelsea House, 2006.

Curie, Ève, and Axel Broe. *Madame Curie.* 1939.

Curie, Marie, et al. *Pierre Curie, by Marie Curie.* Macmillan Co., 1932.

"The Dark Times of Luminous Watches." *CNN*, Cable News Network, 19 Dec. 2017, www.cnn.com/style/article/radium- girls-radioactive-paint/index.html.

Docalavich, Heather, and Shaina Carmel. Indovino. *Poland.* Mason Crest Publishers, 2013.

Guillain, Charlotte. Poland. Heinemann Library, 2012.

"Home." *Famous Scientists*, www.famousscientists.org/irene-joliot-curie/.

"Madame Curie's Passion." *Smithsonian.com*, Smithsonian Institution, 1 Oct. 2011, www.smithsonianmag.com/history/ madame-curies-passion-74183598/#P1RmYmA ycGlCwo0l. 99.

"Marie Curie: From Poland to Paris - BRIEF Exhibit." *Marie Curie: From Poland to Paris - BRIEF Exhibit*, www.aip.org/ history/curie/brief/01_poland/poland_1.html. Accessed 13 Feb. 2013.

McClafferty, Carla Killough. *Something out of Nothing: Marie Curie and Radium.* Farrar Straus Giroux, 2006.

McGrayne, Sharon Bertsch. *Nobel Prize Women in Science: Their Lives, Struggles, and Momentous Discoveries.* Carol Pub. Group, 1993.

Poynter, Margaret. *Marie Curie: Discoverer of Radium.* Enslow, 1994.

SIMMONS, WALTER. POLAND. BLASTOFF READER, 2012.

Venezia, Mike. *Marie Curie: Scientist Who Made Glowing Discoveries.* Children's Press, 2009.

Zuehlke, et al. "Poland in Pictures (Visual Geography. Second Series)." *Biblio - Uncommonly Good Books Found Here.*, Houghton Mifflin, 1 May 2006, www.biblio.com/ 9780822526766.

Cobb, Vicki. *Marie Curie*. DK Publishing, 2008.

Cullen, Katherine E. *Science, Technology, and Society: The People behind the Science*. New York: Chelsea House, 2006.

Krull & Hewitt. *Lives of the scientists: experiments, explosions (and what the neighbors thought)*. New York: Harcourt Children's Books/Houghton Mifflin Harcourt, 2013.

McClafferty, Carla Killough. *Something out of Nothing: Marie Curie and Radium*. New York: Farrar Straus Giroux, 2006.

Venezia, Mike. *Marie Curie: Scientist Who Made Glowing Discoveries (Getting to Know the World's Greatest Inventors & Scientists)*. New York: Children's Press, 2009.

All About... Series

A series for inquisitive young readers

If you liked this book, you may also enjoy:

All About Amelia Earhart*
All About the Appalachian Trail
All About Barack Obama
All About Benjamin Franklin
All About the Brontë Sisters
All About Frederick Douglass
All About the Grand Canyon
All About the Great Lakes
All About Helen Keller
All About Julia Morgan
All About Madam C. J. Walker
All About Mariano River
All About Martin Luther King, Jr.*
All About Mohandas Gandhi
All About Roberto Clemente
All About Sir Edmund Hillary
All About Stephen Curry
All About Stephen Hawking
All About Steve Wozniak
All About Winston Churchill
All About Yellowstone

Also available as an audiobook!

All titles are available in print and ebook form!
Teachers guides and puzzles available at brpressbooks.com/all-about-teachers-guides/